Who Goes Splash?

A ZEBRA BOOK
By Sue Tarsky
Illustrated by Katy Sleight

PUBLISHED BY
WALKER BOOKS
LONDON

Who is climbing?
Who is digging?

Who is watering the garden?
Who is bathing in a puddle?

Who makes muddy footprints?

Who hops?
Who glides along the path?

Who nibbles grass?
Who peeps out of the ground?

Who is hiding in the bushes?

What do you grow
in a vegetable patch?

boot

tomatoes

lettuce

beans

What are the birds eating?
What is the dog eating?

What do you eat in the garden?

What is funny in this garden?

Who is swinging?
Who is sleeping?

Who is running?
Who is sitting on the washing line?

What goes on
the washing line?

What belongs in the sand-pit?

Who likes paddling
in the pool?

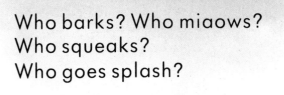

Who barks? Who miaows?
Who squeaks?
Who goes splash?

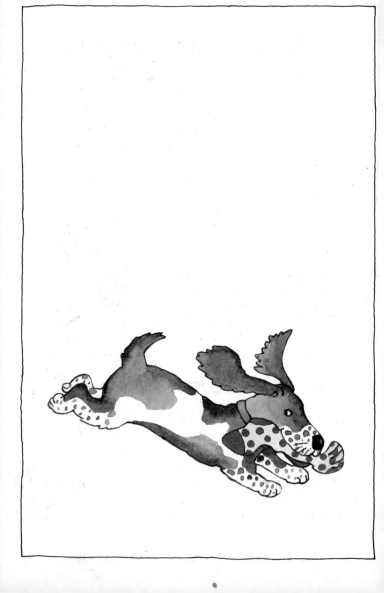